Its References

Citations are added for each entry for two reasons:

First, in our era of too many false narratives about our history, it is an effort to document real historical events from recognized sources. Since this is a 'speaker's guide' and not a history text, the sources are an *introduction* to the evidence behind the event. We invite you to delve deeper, for deeper reflection.

Second, some citations offer additional information which might help you focus your speech or stir an interest in a related topic.

Its Potential Follow-up Questions for Each Entry

- Why did this event happen?
- And why did this event happen *when* it did?
- What is our initial response to this event?
- What are we thinking, feeling, or imagining?
- What social, personal, religious, political (and more) factors propelled this event?
- What can we learn from this past event, for the benefit of our future?

Tunes for the Times, Then and Now
Songs, Smiles, Reducing Stress, Billie Holiday

On January 6, 1938, Billie Holiday recorded *When You're Smiling, the Whole World Smiles With You*, for *Teddy Wilson and His Orchestra.*

Research on brain and behavior indicates that certain endorphins and neurotransmitters are released when smiling, and also while singing, reducing stress and even depression.

African slaves who sang hopeful songs while laboring in America under horrific circumstances, were not singing because they were happy, but hoping for, and perhaps actually finding relief for their pain.

Billie Holiday: 4/7/1915 – 7/17/1959

https://billieholiday.com/

https://pubmed.ncbi.nlm.nih.gov/35285408/

https://www.hopkinsallchildrens.org/Patients-Families/Health-Library/HealthDocNew/Good-Reasons-to-Smile

https://www.bbc.com/future/article/20200518-why-singing-can-make-you-feel-better-in-lockdown

Challenges At Ground Level,
As Well As *Above* Ground Level
Mountain Explorer, Mount Everest,
Challenges, Goals, Edmund Hillary

Sir Edmund Hillary, who died on January 11, 2008, was a pioneering mountaineer and explorer who faced many challenges as he and a guide were the first to reach the peak of Mount Everest.

But he had previously faced challenges as early as grammar school.

His mother was dissatisfied with Edmund's mediocre grammar school grades, and she wanted him to attend a better school. To get to the new school, he had to bicycle for an hour and forty minutes to catch a train for the rest of the commute. And then return the same way!

Sir Edmund Hillary: 7/20/1919 – 1/11/2008

https://en.wikipedia.org/wiki/Edmund_Hillary

The Origin of Common Practices
Now-Common Department Store Features.
Origins, Customer, Display,
The "Bargain Basement", Marshall Field

Marshall Field was an American entrepreneur, philanthropist, and the founder of a chain of department stores bearing his name. Though he died on January 16, 1906, his innovations have endured into the present.

Among them, he is credited with the slogan, "the customer is always right", introduced the front-window display of merchandise to draw pedestrians in, opened a restaurant inside the store; *and* introduced *the bargain basement*.

He set more trends, even including moving his business locations to sections of the city which were, at the time, more easily accessible to women.

Marshall Field: 8/18/1834 – 1/16/1906

https://www.encyclopedia.com/people/social-sciences-and-law/business-leaders/marshall-field

Driving Forces of Life, Lasting to the End
Mental States, Treatment, Scientific Investigations, George Miller Beard

George Miller Beard was a neurologist with a significant interest in psychiatry, and he became a major contributor to advances in understanding and treating unhealthy mental states.

His investigative mind was still focused on these interests, even on his deathbed, on January 23, 1883.

Among his final words were, "It is impossible to record the thoughts of a dying man. It would be interesting to do so, but I cannot. My time has come. I hope others will carry on my work."

George M. Beard: 5/8/1839 – 1/23/1883

Exits: Stories of Dying Moments & Parting Words, by Scott Slater & Alec Solomita

https://archives.yale.edu/repositories/12/resources/3104

A Television First for Women
Women, Diversity, Arts, Radio, Television, Soap Operas, Irna Phillips

On January 31, 1949, the first daytime *soap opera* in American television appeared on NBC. It was called *These Are My Children*.

The new project was short-lived, lasting for less than two months.

But its producer and writer, the trailblazing Irna Phillips had a long-lived and influential career in radio and TV programs.

Her resume included the creation of *As the World Turns*, which aired for 54 years and *The Guiding Light,* which aired for 57 years.

Irna Phillips: 7/1/1901 – 12/23/1973

https://blogs.loc.gov/now-see-hear/2022/03/the-queen-of-soaps-speaks-for-herself/

Our *Words* Can Influence Our *Thinking*
Words, Thinking, Behavior, Sapir-Whorf, Edward Sapir

Edward Sapir, who died on February 4, 1939, was an anthropologist and linguist known for the study of indigenous North and South American languages, and a major contributor to *The Sapir-Whorf Hypothesis*, which proposed that *how we speak* influences *how we think*, not just the reverse.

For example, using inclusive *language* can foster inclusive *thinking*, and using *exclusive* language can result in *exclusive* thinking.

And, naturally, our *thinking* influences our *actions*.

Words really *do* matter.

Edward Sapir: 1/26/1884 – 2/4/1939

https://www.britannica.com/biography/Edward-Sapir

Picture It
Pictures, Photography, Civil War, Matthew Brady

On February 9, 1864, Matthew Brady, the well-known American photographer, captured the image of a calmly posed Abraham Lincoln. That photograph was later selected for the face of the $5 bill in American currency.

If you have ever seen real-time photographs of the American Civil War, or portraits of civilians, or military and political leaders of that era, you have likely seen his work.

His images of war and of mid-19th century America were seared into the public mind.

Matthew Brady: ? – 1/15/1896

https://www.loc.gov/collections/civil-war-glass-negatives/articles-and-essays/mathew-brady-biographical-note/

Working Together
Writing, Hollywood,
Collaboration, Pelham Wodehouse

Sir Pelham Grenville Wodehouse, who died on February 14, 1975, was an English author and humorist who wrote novels and movie scripts.

Working in Hollywood, he is credited with reflecting, "The actual work is negligible…"

"So far, I have had eight collaborators. The system is that A. gets the original idea, B. comes in to work with him on it, C. makes a scenario, D. does preliminary dialogue, and then they send for me to insert [aspects of] class and what-not. Then E. and F., scenario writers, alter the plot and off we go again."

Working together can sometimes be a challenge.

Pelham Wodehouse: 10/15/1881- 2/14/1975

https://en.wikipedia.org/wiki/P._G._Wodehouse

http://henrybemisbookseller.blogspot.com/2015/10/birthday-aside-from-his-writing-pg.html

From Literature to Science
Interdisciplinary, Fiction, Diagnosis, Munchausen Syndrome, Baron Munchausen, Erich Raspe, Richard Asher,

Baron Karl Munchausen, who died on February 22, 1797, was known for his much embellished tales of world travels.

He was the inspiration for a book by Erich Raspe, a contemporary of the Baron, and a librarian and writer.

Raspe's book described a fictional version of Munchausen, who was self-abusive in order to receive the attention of care-givers.

Over a century later, Richard Asher, an eminent British medical doctor and researcher, identified the *Munchausen Syndrome,* partly based on Raspe's character.

From an actual figure in history, to a fictional character in literature, to a medical discovery – sometimes new insights develop through many interdisciplinary links.

Karl Munchausen: 5/11/1720 – 2/22/1797
https://en.wikipedia.org/wiki/Baron_Munchausen

Erich Raspe: 3/?/1720 – 11/16/1794
https://en.wikipedia.org/wiki/Rudolf_Erich_Raspe

Richard Asher: 4/3/1912 – 4/25/1969
https://en.wikipedia.org/wiki/Richard_Asher

NOTES

An Edited Shakespearean Play
Actor, Playwright,
William Shakespeare, Colley Cibber

On March 5, 1750, the first American production of a play by William Shakespeare was presented in New York City.

However, though advertised as *Richard III* by Shakespeare, the script was heavily edited and adapted by a not-so-successful playwright, Colley Cibber.

The Cibber version was called a "hodge podge" of lines from *Richard III* and other Shakespeare plays, even with added lines written by Cibber himself.

His script-writing career was much aligned by his contemporary, Alexander Pope.

Cibber's autobiography was titled, *An Apology for the Life of Colley Cibber, Comedian.*

Colley Cibber: 11/6/1671 – 12/11/1757

Famous First Facts, *5th Edition*. Joseph Nathan Kane, Steven Anzovin, Janet Podell, page 20.

https://en.wikipedia.org/wiki/Colley_Cibber

A Dramatic Event
Broadway, African American,
Best Play Award, Lorraine Hansberry

When *A Raisin in the Sun,* written by Lorraine Hansberry, opened in New York City on March 11, 1959, it became the first play by an African American woman to be performed on Broadway.

In 1959, the author also became the youngest American playwright to win the New York Drama Critics' Circle *Best Play Award.* The play was nominated for four Tony Awards.

Perhaps because the award-winning cast was all Black, except one, and the script was by a Black woman, it took over a year to raise the funds for the production. The successful film version was produced two years later.

(See the January 12 entry for a different aspect in her life and work.)

Lorraine Hansberry: 5/19/1930 – 1/12/1965

https://en.wikipedia.org/wiki/Lorraine_Hansberry

A First in Electoral Ballots
Diversity, Women, Vice President, Politics, Theodora Nathan

Theodora Nathan, who died on March 20, 2014, was the first Jewish person *and* the first woman to receive an electoral ballot for Vice President in the United States, cast on January 6, 1973.

She was a member of the Libertarian Party.

Theodora Nathan: 2/9/1923 – 3/20/2014

https://awpc.cattcenter.iastate.edu/directory/theodora-tonie-nathan/

https://www.nytimes.com/1973/01/07/archives/its-official-nixon-won-520-to-17.html

Luck (and Hard Work)
Luck, Hard Work, Stephen Butler Leacock

Stephen Butler Leacock, who died on March 28, 1944, was a Canadian teacher, political scientist, economist and humorist.

He once observed, "I am a great believer in luck, and I find the harder I work, the more I have *of* it."

Stephen Butler Leacock: 12/30/1869 – 3/28/1944

https://www.cbc.ca/comedy/6-stephen-leacock-quotes-that-still-shock-1.4429160

https://en.wikipedia.org/wiki/Stephen_Leacock

When applied to a belief that gravity is not real, or the earth is flat, or the sun revolves around the earth, that definition applies.

But there is another definition of myth: a story about something that never *really* happened but is *always* happening.

This definition is understood by theologians, philosophers and writers.

Shakespeare's story of Romeo and Juliet, or for that matter, *all* of Shakespeare's plays, are about fictional characters who never lived, but whose experiences are *always* happening.

Charlie Brown's experience of being fooled every football season in that famous *Peanuts* cartoon never *really* happened, but is *always* happening around us.

Any Agatha Christie novel about a fictional murder can tell a story which never really happened but could *always* happen.

Aesop's Fables, Kahlil Gibran's *The Prophet*, and classic literature is mythology filled with truth, told through stories of fictional characters.

But then, the storyteller begins to explain that the mystery of what happened in the story was not really a mystery after all, offering an application of scientific investigation.

Imagine a lifelong smoker and consequent lung-cancer patient is facing death in hospice care, hoping to find a peaceful end.

But then, a friend or relative visits to lecture that there is now no mystery about the consequences of smoking.

Imagine that there is a genetic test which could reveal the probability of developing an incapacitating disease in the future.

Would you want to solve the mystery and take that test now?

Imagine a person who has survived a painful experience, such as a near-death scare, an abuse, or a divorce.

One person might *not* want to de-mystify the experience, since it may be a difficult journey of self-discovery, while another might *want* to de-mystify the experience in order to control the future.

NOTES